Developing Optimism

Teaching Children the Value of Positive Thinking

by W. A. R. Boyer, Ph.D.
and Barb Rumson

Fearon Teacher Aids

A Division of Frank Schaffer Publications, Inc.

Body Illustrations: Megan Jeffery and Steve Sullivan
Cover Illustration: Jeanette Courtin

Editors: Cindy Barden, Janet Barker, Hanna Otero, Christine Hood
Cover Design: Riley Wilkinson
Interior Design: Riley Wilkinson
Digital Prepress: Carol Arriola, Drew R. Moore

Fearon Teacher Aids products were formerly manufactured and distributed by American Teaching Aids, Inc., a subsidiary of Silver Burdett Ginn, and are now manufactured and distributed by Frank Schaffer Publications, Inc. FEARON, FEARON TEACHER AIDS, and the FEARON balloon logo are marks used under license from Simon & Schuster, Inc.

FE11026 Developing Optimism — Grades K-1
© **Fearon Teacher Aids**
A Division of Frank Schaffer Publications, Inc.
23740 Hawthorne Boulevard
Torrance, CA 90505-5927

Table of Contents

Introduction 4

Lesson 1
The Magical Talking Stick..................5
The Magical Talking Stick Script 6
Discussion Questions 7
Extension Activities........................8
The Tree with the Magical Talking Stick 9

Lesson 2
The Magical Talking Stick
Points the Way 10–11
The Magical Talking Stick Chart Story.............12–13
The Magical Talking Stick Rules 14
Extension Activities 15

Lesson 3
Emotion Detectives..................16–18
Discussion Questions 19
Happy Boy and Girl;
Grumpy Boy and Girl Pictures 20
Extension Activities.......................21

Lesson 4
Clap Your Hands! Shout Hurray! 22–24
Extension Activities.......................25

Lesson 5
What Is an Optimist? 26–27
Duck and Bear Go to the Movies Story.........28
Flannelboard Patterns 29–30
Discussion Questions 31
Extension Activities.......................31

Lesson 6
Winning Words—I Can 32–33
Extension Activities.......................33
"Can You Do It?" Song 34

Lesson 7
Winning Words—I'm Sorry 35
Extension Activities.......................36
"I Am Sorry" Song 37

Lesson 8
Winning Words—I Am Thankful.............38–39
Extension Activities.......................39
"I Am Thankful" Song 40

Lesson 9
People Puzzles 41–43
Discussion Questions 42–43
People Puzzle Pictures 44–47
Extension Activities.......................48

Lesson 10
Laugh a Lot 49–50
"I Can Make Me Laugh" Chant 51
Extension Activities.......................52

Lesson 11
Dessert Duos 53–55
Extension Activities.......................56

Lesson 12
Cheery Chums......................57
Discussion Questions 58
Cheery Chums Script 59–60
Extension Activities.......................61

Lesson 13
Welcome to the Cheery Chums
Optimist Club 62
Cheery Chums Optimist Club Pledge 63
Cheery Chums Optimist Club Certificate 64

Introduction

Our society is constantly faced with innovation, change, and challenge. To cope positively with the unexpected, children should be prepared to identify, create, and embrace opportunities for learning and fulfillment. To do this, each child needs self-confidence and an optimistic point of view.

When faced with challenges, children, like adults, may need help to combat apprehension, self-doubt, and rigidity, which could result in stagnation and personal defeat.

Developing Optimism presents 13 complete lesson plans to help you provide a framework for children to develop a positive attitude toward life. Each unit includes a detailed, motivating presentation with objectives, a materials list, and an approximation of the time needed for each part of the lesson. You'll also find handouts, patterns, discussion questions, and student reproducibles. Pages also provide space for you to make notes to enhance your presentation.

Following each lesson are easy-to-use cross-curricular extension activities. These art, music, science, math, social studies, and language arts ideas will help you extend and reinforce concepts learned in each lesson. A list of related reading material is also included.

As you join children in songs, stories, role-play, and more, you will encourage them to develop self-confidence and find ways to take an optimist approach to life.

Developing Optimism will change your classroom dynamics by shifting the focus from negative to positive, from pessimistic to optimistic. As the title of Lesson 10 implies, you and your students will "laugh a lot" as you learn that a sunny disposition is wonderfully contagious.

The Magical Talking Stick

Materials

"The Magical Talking Stick Script" (page 6)

tree branch

globe

art materials for selected activities

Objective: Children will realize the importance of taking turns while speaking in group situations.

Time: Approximately 15–20 minutes *(Additional time may be needed depending on extension activities selected.)*

2 minutes	**Introduction**	**Teacher:** "A fable is a story that explains something about the world we live in or teaches us a lesson. Did you ever hear the story about the lion and the mouse? That is a fable that tells us how friends can help each other.

"Today we are going to read a very important fable. Listen carefully to the story. What lesson does this fable teach us?" |
| **7** minutes | **Read/Listen** | *Read "The Magical Talking Stick Script." As you read, emphasize hand gestures and theatrical voicing appropriate to various parts of the story. Suggestions are included in the script. Feel free to add your own ideas.* |
| **10** minutes | **Anchoring** | *Use the questions at the end of the story for group discussion. If children all begin to talk at once, remind them of the Magical Talking Stick.* |

The Magical Talking Stick Script

Narrator: *(pointing to globe)* When the earth was first created, women, men, and children had problems talking with one another. Everyone wanted to talk first and longest. No one wanted to let others speak. The noise was unbearable.

(Cover your ears to show how loud it was.)

Narrator: Nearby, a large, tall tree stood to protect the people.

(Stand and pretend to be a large tree. Hold the tree branch with one hand.)

Narrator: The tree did not like all the noise and confusion.

(Frown to show that the tree is unhappy.)

Narrator: Finally, the tree could stand the noise no longer. The tree began to shake and rumble in anger. The tree's roots shook the ground.

(Demonstrate by moving the branch back and forth. Then sit to continue reading the story.)

Narrator: All the women, men, and children stopped talking. They looked up at the tree.

(Gaze upward at "the tree.")

Narrator: They heard a whispering through the leaves of the tree. Everyone strained their ears to hear what the tree was saying.

(Tilt your head as though listening.)

Narrator: The leaves of the tall tree crackled and fluttered. The branches swayed, although there was no wind. A rustling voice whispered from the tree:

(Stand as the tree again. Hold the branch. Speak in a rustling, whispery voice.)

Narrator: "We all need to speak. We all need to be listened to. But only one person must speak at a time. The rest of you must listen. I will give you a part of myself to help you remember this."

(Drop the tree branch. Then pick up the branch again and continue talking as the tree.)

Narrator: "This will be your Magical Talking Stick. This Magical Talking Stick gives the person holding it the right and opportunity to speak. I give you this stick as a sign of peace."

(Hold out the branch as though offering it to the children.)

Narrator: "If you receive the Magical Talking Stick and do not wish to speak, that is your right. If you choose to speak, you have a responsibility to speak words of beauty. You do not have the right to speak ugly words. The Magical Talking Stick will be passed from person to person."

The people thanked the tree for giving them a way to end the noise and confusion.

Discussion Questions

After reading "The Magical Talking Stick Script," extend the lesson by presenting the following questions in group discussion.

1. What were the men, women, and children doing that made so much noise?

2. How did the tree feel about all the noise and confusion?

3. What did the tree do to get the people's attention?

4. Why did the tree decide to speak to the people?

5. What were some of the suggestions whispered by the tree?

6. What did the tree give the people to help them?

7. What were the rules of the Magical Talking Stick?
   (Write these on chart paper as the children say them.)

8. If you were the tree, what would you have said?
   (Write children's ideas on a separate sheet of chart paper.)

9. How do you think the rules of the Magical Talking Stick can help us when we are in a large group?

10. How do you think the rules of the Magical Talking Stick can be used even when there are fewer people?

11. Words can be ugly when they hurt someone's feelings. How do you feel when you hear ugly words?

12. Kind words are words of beauty. How do you feel when you hear kind words?

13. How does it make you feel when you do not get a chance to speak?

14. How do you feel when you do get a chance to speak?

15. How can we use these rules in our classroom?

16. Are these rules fair to everyone? Why?

17. Where else can we use these rules?

18. Do we need a Magical Talking Stick to follow these rules?

19. Is that the only time we should follow these rules?

20. Are these good rules? Why, or why not?

Extension Activities

These activities have been designed to extend the learning opportunities in Lesson 1. They can easily be adapted into most lesson plans, using one or more suggestions each day or throughout the week. By weaving the concepts learned in Lesson 1 throughout the curriculum, students will have a better understanding of the story and how it relates to other facets of their lives.

Art

Have children draw the tall tree from "The Magical Talking Stick." Next, have them draw the part of the story they liked best. Encourage children to work in small groups to design and decorate their own Magical Talking Sticks. Give each group a small branch and items for decoration, such as paper leaves cut from construction paper or wallpaper, glitter, string, yarn, aluminum foil, bric-a-brac, and lace.

Math

Make copies of "The Tree With the Magical Talking Stick" reproducible (page 9). Help children count sequentially to connect the dots. Then encourage them to color their trees.

Language Arts

- Ask children to retell "The Magical Talking Stick" to a family member. When they return to class, ask: "What did your family member(s) think of the story?" Allow each student to share with the class.
- Write a group story as a sequel to "The Magical Talking Stick." Have children sit in a circle. Create a new Magical Talking Stick story. The class version could be about someone who does not remember the rules of the Magical Talking Stick and what the tree does to (gently) help the child remember. Have each student add one sentence to the story, going around the circle. Tape-record or write the story as he or she tells it. Print the new story on chart paper and read it to the class.

Related Reading

The Baby Train and Other Lusty Urban Legends by Jan H. Brunvand (Norton, 1993).
The Bundle of Sticks, an Aesop's fable found in many collections.
The Giving Tree by Shel Silverstein (Harper, 1964).
The Last Eagle by B. East (Crown, 1974).
Long-Tailed Bear by N. M. Belting (Bobs Merril, 1961).

Name_____

The Tree with the Magical Talking Stick

Connect the dots to find the tree that gave people the Magical Talking Stick. Then color the tree.

The Magical Talking Stick Points the Way

Materials

"The Magical Talking Stick" story (pages 12 and 13) Display the story on an easel or chart board.

"Magical Talking Stick Rules" (page 14), one copy per child

art materials for selected activities

Objective: Children will understand the benefits of taking turns when speaking.

Time: Approximately 25–30 minutes
(Additional time may be needed depending on extension activities selected.)

Time	Activity	Procedure
5 minutes	Introduction	**Teacher:** "Please sit in a circle with only your knees touching. We will be spending time together and talking. There are some rules we must follow when we talk. If we follow these rules, everyone will get a chance to talk and it will be fun." *Allow children time to arrange themselves so that only their knees are touching.* **Teacher:** "In our last lesson, we learned about the Magical Talking Stick. The wise old tree gave the people some good rules to help them communicate with one another. Who knows what *communicate* means?" *Pause and allow several children to give their definitions of communicate.* **Teacher:** "That's right. To *communicate* means to talk with other people and listen to other people. Both talking and listening are important to communicate."

The Magical Talking Stick Points the Way

Time	Activity	Procedure
8 minutes	**Read Together**	*Read "The Magical Talking Stick" as a group.* *Point to each word as you read. Encourage children to read along and add appropriate actions to the story.*
8 minutes	**Discussion**	*Ask children about the communication rules they learned about in the story.* *When they have remembered all the rules, give each child a copy of "Magical Talking Stick Rules." Read the rules again together. Ask children to write their names on their Magical Talking Sticks. Explain that this page is like a contract, a promise to remember and use the rules.*
5 minutes	**Anchoring**	**Teacher:** "How can these rules help us in our classroom? "Where else can these rules be used? "What was your favorite part of the story 'The Magical Talking Stick'?" *Display a copy of "Magical Talking Stick Rules" on the classroom bulletin board.*

Name _____

The Magical Talking Stick

When the earth was first created, women, men, and children had problems talking with one another. Everyone wanted to talk first and longest. No one wanted to let others speak. The noise was unbearable.

Nearby, a large, tall tree stood to protect the people. The tree did not like all the noise and confusion. Finally, the tree could stand the noise no longer. The tree began to shake and rumble in anger. The tree's roots shook the ground.

All the women, men, and children stopped talking. They looked up at the tree.

They heard a whispering through the leaves of the tall tree. Everyone strained their ears to hear what the tree was saying. The leaves of the tall tree crackled and fluttered.

The branches swayed, although there was no wind.

A rustling voice whispered from the tree:

"We all need to speak. We all need to be listened to. But only one person must speak at a time. The rest of you must listen.

"I will give you a part of myself to help you remember this. This will be your Magical Talking Stick.

"This Magical Talking Stick gives the person holding it the right and opportunity to speak.

"I give you this stick as a sign of peace.

"If you receive the Magical Talking Stick and do not wish to speak, that is your right.

"If you choose to speak, you have a responsibility to speak words of beauty. You do not have the right to speak ugly words.

"The Magical Talking Stick will be passed from person to person."

The people thanked the tree for giving them a way to end the noise and confusion.

Name_____

Magical Talking Stick Rules

1. We all have to take turns.

2. Whoever has the Magical Talking Stick has the right to speak.

3. The Magical Talking Stick is passed from person to person.

4. If you choose not to speak, pass the Magical Talking Stick to the next person.

5. We will use only kind words.

     reproducible

Extension Activities

Art

• Encourage children to color their Magical Talking Stick Rules. Have them draw themselves in the picture. Each child can take this page home to share with his or her family.

• Have students draw pictures of people in different situations using the rules learned from the Magical Talking Stick. These situations can include the classroom, on the playground, while playing a game, in a restaurant, and at home.

Language Arts

Have children look through old magazines for pictures of people following the rules of the Magical Talking Stick. Ask them to make up short stories about the pictures and share them with the class.

Science

Use Lesson 2 in conjunction with a science unit on trees, leaves, plants, or seeds. Help children see the connection between the story and science by speculating about the tree's species. Although the story is fiction, ask children, "What could cause a tree to shake in real life?"

Bulletin Board Display

Display the large-print copy of "The Magical Talking Stick" story along with a copy of "Magical Talking Stick Rules." Add student artwork to the display, as well as collections of leaves and seeds. You may want to

create a tree as the center of the display. To do this, twist sheets of brown butcher paper into a trunk and branches. Add construction-paper leaves and flowers to the tree.

Related Reading

Aesop's Fables by Aesop (Jellybean, 1988).

Backyard Games by A. Cort Sinnes (Andrews, 1993).

Eric Carle's Treasury of Classic Stories for Children by Aesop, Hans Christian Andersen, and the Brothers Grimm. Edited by Eric Carle (Watts, 1988).

Hopscotch, Hangman, Hot Potato, and Ha, Ha, Ha's: A Rulebook of Children's Games by Jack Maguire (Prentice-Hall, 1990).

Perfect Pigs: An Introduction to Manners by Marc Brown and Stephen Krensky (Little, 1983).

Emotion Detectives

Materials

happy boy and girl picture (page 20)

grumpy boy and girl picture (page 20)

"Magical Talking Stick Rules" (page 14)

art materials for selected activities

Objectives: Children will explore their happy and grumpy feelings.
Children will look for ways to help overcome grumpy feelings.

Time: Approximately 15–20 minutes
(Additional time may be needed depending on extension activities selected.)

Time	Activity	Procedure
5 minutes	**Introduction**	*Display a copy of "Magical Talking Stick Rules." Invite children to sit in a circle.* **Teacher:** "Thumbs up if you remember the rules of the Magical Talking Stick." *Demonstrate "thumbs up" and wait for children's responses.* **Teacher:** "Thank you. That's great. Let's read the rules together." *Point to the rules as you read them with the class.* **Teacher:** "We will need these rules for today's activity. Today we are going to be Emotion Detectives. Do you know what a detective does?" *Wait for children's responses.* **Teacher:** "A detective is a person who finds solutions to mysteries. Today we will all be detectives. We are going to find out who is happy and who is grumpy." *Hold up the picture of the happy boy and girl.*

Emotion Detectives

Time	Activity	Procedure
		Teacher: "Who is happy in this picture? Is this girl happy? Is this boy happy? How can you tell they are happy?" *Wait for children's responses.* **Teacher:** "How many of you have ever had a happy day?" *Wait for a show of hands. Hopefully, all children will indicate they have had happy days.* **Teacher:** "What kinds of things make you happy?" *You can start by telling about something that makes you happy. Allow several children to respond. Write their answers on the chalkboard under the heading* Happy. *Keep a copy of this list to use in Lesson 4.* **Teacher:** "Can you give an example of a time when you were happy?" *Encourage several children to give specific examples. Hold up the picture of the grumpy boy and girl.* **Teacher:** "Who is grumpy in this picture?" *Wait for children's responses.* **Teacher:** "You are all great emotion detectives! How can you tell they are grumpy? How many of you have ever had a grumpy day?" *Wait for a show of hands. Most children will probably admit that they have had grumpy days.* **Teacher:** "What kinds of things make you feel grumpy?"

Emotion Detectives

Time	Activity	Procedure
	Introduction (continued)	*You can start by telling about something that makes you grumpy. Encourage several children to respond. Write their answers on the chalkboard under the heading* Grumpy. *Keep a copy of this list to use in Lesson 4.* **Teacher:** "Can you give an example of a time when you were grumpy?" *Encourage several children to give specific examples. Some children will mix up grumpy with sad or angry. The difference will be discussed later in this lesson.* **Teacher:** "Raise your hands if you are happy today." *Wait for a show of hands. Comment on the results:* "It's great to see so many of you are happy" *or* "It looks like a few of you aren't having a very happy day." **Teacher:** "Raise your hands if you are grumpy today." *Wait for a show of hands. Comment on how good it is that so few are grumpy, or show concern that some seem to be having a grumpy day.*
10 minutes	**Discussion**	**Teacher:** "Now let's solve another mystery." *Use the questions on page 19 for group discussion.*
2 minutes	**Anchoring**	**Teacher:** "Sometimes it helps to smile and say, 'I'm very happy today.' When you're grumpy, try saying this three times. It can't hurt, and it just might help. "If that doesn't help, try some of the other grumpy-chasing ideas we talked about today."

Discussion Questions

1. Why are we happy?

2. How do we show that we're happy?

3. Let's talk about why some of us are grumpy today. Why are we grumpy?

4. How do we show that we're grumpy?

5. Which feels better: being happy or being grumpy? Thumbs up if you're happy. Thumbs down if you're grumpy.

6. How do you feel when you are around people who are happy?

7. How do people around us feel when we're happy?

8. How do you feel when you are around people who are grumpy?

9. How do people around us feel when we're grumpy?

10. Is grumpy the same as sad?

11. Is it OK to be sad?

   (Explain that everyone is sad sometimes. Being sad is not bad, but it makes us feel better when we can get over our sad feelings.)

12. Is grumpy the same as angry?

13. How are grumpy and angry different?

14. Is it OK to be angry?

   (Explain that everyone is angry sometimes. Being angry is not bad, but if we break something, hurt someone, or hurt ourselves because we are angry, then it is not good.)

15. Why is it better for us to try to feel happy?

16. Let's talk about some ways to chase away the "grumpies." How can we get over our grumpy feelings?

   (Write children's ideas on the board under the heading Grumpy Chasers. Encourage children to suggest talking to parents, teachers, or friends to get over grumpiness, or doing something that makes them happy, such as reading a book, watching a favorite movie, or playing with a favorite toy.)

reproducible

Extension Activities

Art
- Help children make "Happy Gardens." They can cut flower parts (petals, circles, stems, leaves) from wallpaper scraps or colored construction paper. Have them glue the circles on white construction paper, add colored flower petals, stems, and leaves to make several flowers. Ask children to draw happy faces in the circles. On the petals, help them write "happy" words—things that make them happy. Display the Happy Gardens on a bulletin board.
- Demonstrate how to fold a sheet of construction paper in half. On the front of their papers, have children draw gray clouds with grumpy faces. On the clouds, have them write: *I am grumpy when . . . .* Help them fill in words or phrases to finish the sentence. Then have children open the papers. On the inside, have them draw white clouds with happy faces. On the clouds, have them write: *I get happy by . . . .* Help children fill in a words or phrases to finish the sentence.

Language Arts
- Have each child cut out a picture of a happy person and a grumpy person from old magazines, then glue each picture on a separate sheet of paper. Ask children to explain why they think the people are happy or grumpy. Have them share their stories at circle time.
- Give each child a sheet of paper with *I'm happy when . . .* printed across the top. Ask children to write or draw several endings for the sentence and share their creations at circle time.

Related Reading
ABC Book of Feelings by Marlys Moddy (Concordia, 1991).
Alexander and the Terrible, Horrible, No Good, Very Bad Day by Judith Viorst (Macmillan, 1972).
Badger's Bad Mood by Oram Hiawyn (Scholastic, 1998).
The Berenstain Bears Get the Grouchies by Stan Berenstain (Inchworm, 1997).
Feeling Angry (Let's Talk About) by Maggie Smith (Scholastic, 1996).
Feelings by Aliki (Greenwillow, 1984).
The Frog with the Grumpy Jump by Helen Piper Miller (Mountain House, 1997).

Clap Your Hands!
Shout Hurray!

Materials

2 craft sticks per child

glue or tape

two 2-inch (5-cm) circles per child

crayons or markers

happy and grumpy lists from Lesson 3

art materials for selected activities

Objectives: Children will explore their happy and grumpy feelings.
Children will look for ways to help overcome grumpy feelings.

Time: Approximately 15–20 minutes
(Additional time may be needed depending on extension activities selected.)

Time	Activity	Procedure
5 minutes	**Introduction**	*Sing "If You're Happy and You Know It." Encourage children to join in singing the words and doing the accompanying actions. Encourage them to use happy, enthusiastic voices.* **Teacher:** "I can see by the expressions on your faces that you are happy today. Did you know that our expressions give other people a message? Others can tell from our faces if we are happy or grumpy." *Make a happy face. Ask children to look at the expression on your face and explain how they think you feel. Then make a grumpy face and ask them to explain how they think you feel when you have that expression.* **Teacher:** "Today we are going to play a game about happy and grumpy expressions. Our game is called *Face Up.*"

Clap Your Hands! Shout Hurray!

Time	Activity	Procedure
5 minutes	**Craft**	*Give each child two 2-inch (5-cm) construction-paper circles, two craft sticks, glue or tape, and crayons or markers. Ask him or her to draw a happy face on one circle and a grumpy face on the other. Have children write their names on the backs of the circles.* *Demonstrate how to glue or tape the faces to the end craft sticks. Ask children to hold one craft stick in each hand.*
10 minutes	**Role-Play**	**Teacher:** "Now you're ready to play the game *Face Up.* When I say the word *happy,* raise the stick with the happy face. When I say the word *grumpy,* raise the stick with the grumpy face. Let's try it." *Say the words* happy *and* grumpy *a few times while children raise the correct faces.* **Teacher:** "Now raise the stick with the correct face to answer the questions. "Can you show me which face makes us feel good? "Which face makes other people happy? "Which face makes other people grumpy? "Which face makes us look friendly? "Which face makes us want to clap our hands and sing? "Great!" *(Give a thumbs up.)* "Now let's try another part of the game. "Which face shows how we feel when we get a nice surprise?

Clap Your Hands! Shout Hurray!

Time	Activity	Procedure
	Role-Play (continued)	"Which face shows how we feel when we see other people smiling? "Which face shows how we feel when we can't do something we want to do, like not being able to go on a picnic because it is raining? "How could we change our grumpy faces to happy faces if that happened?" *Encourage children to mention other fun things they could do instead.* *Continue the game. Use the lists you made in Lesson 3 of things that make children happy or grumpy. For each thing that makes children grumpy, encourage them to offer suggestions on how to turn those feelings around. Give them some suggestions.*
2 minutes	**Anchoring**	*Sing "If You're Happy and You Know It" enthusiastically with children. Then ask them to show you which face best illustrates how they feel now.* *Close the lesson with a positive comment about how great it is to see so many happy faces. Collect their craft-stick faces and save them for the next lesson.*

Extension Activities

Art

- Give children several three-inch (7.5-cm) circles cut from different-colored construction paper. Ask them to decorate these "faces" with different expressions. Use the completed faces as a border on your bulletin board.

- On large sheets of paper, have children draw two faces. On one face, have them write the word h $_a$ $_p$ ^{p} y in the shape of a smile. On the other, they can write the word g ^{r} ^{u} ^{m} $_p$ y in the shape of a frown. Invite them to draw other facial features (eyes, nose, ears, eyebrows) or write the corresponding words in the shape of each feature.

- Have children decorate several two-inch (5-cm) circles with happy faces to make ornaments. Punch a hole at the top of each face with a hole punch. Provide yarn, string, or ribbon to make hangers for children to make happy-face ornaments. Place your Magical Talking Stick branch in a coffee can partly filled with sand or small stones to keep it upright. Encourage children hang their happy-face ornaments from the branch.

Language Arts

- Encourage children to transform their happy- and grumpy-face craft sticks into puppets. Ask them to work with partners to tell short stories using their puppets.

- Have children draw large happy faces. Around the outside of the faces, they can write "happy words" in different colors, such as *warm day, blue sky, holiday, hot dogs, pizza, presents,* and *birthday.*

Related Reading

Crossing a New Bridge by E. McCully (Putnam, 1994).
Duck, Duck, Goose? by Katya Arnold (Holiday House, 1997).
1,400 Things for Kids to Be Happy About: The Happy Book by Barbara Ann Kipfer (Workman, 1994).
The Grouchy Ladybug by Eric Carle (Demco Media, 1996).

What Is an Optimist?

Materials

craft-stick faces from Lesson 4

"Duck and Bear Go to the Movies" story (page 28)

flannelboard character patterns (pages 29 and 30)

art materials for selected activities

Objectives: Children will learn what it means to be an optimist.
Children will identify story characters who are optimistic.

Time: Approximately 15–20 minutes
(Additional time may be needed depending on extension activities selected.)

Time	Activity	Procedure
5 minutes	**Introduction**	**Teacher:** "Would everyone please show me a happy smile? Great. It makes me feel good when I see your smiling faces. "Today we are going to learn a new word for people who are happy most of the time. Can you think of any words that mean the same as *happy*?" *Let children suggest several synonyms. Then write the word* optimist *on the board and pronounce it for them.* **Teacher:** "An optimist is a person who is happy most of the time. An optimist looks for things to be happy about, even when it isn't such a great day. "Do you think you can remember this new word for a happy person? Let's say it together—*optimist.* Show me your happy-face puppets. Are your puppets optimists? "Have you ever watched a movie or read a story about Winnie-the-Pooh? Which character is called Eyeore?"

What Is an Optimist?

Time	Activity	Procedure
		Wait for response that Eeyore is the donkey. **Teacher:** "Is Eeyore an optimist?" *(No.)* "Why not?" *(Because he is always gloomy.)* "Can you name any characters in books or movies who are optimists?" *Let children name some characters who are optimists. Ask them to give examples of situations in which these characters were optimistic. Write the names of the characters on the board.* **Teacher:** "How about Charlotte, the spider, in E. B. White's *Charlotte's Web?*" *Name other characters in stories you've read in class. Ask children if those characters are optimists.*
5 minutes	Read/Listen	*Read "Duck and Bear Go to the Movies" to the class. Use the patterns on pages 29 and 30 to cut out pieces for a flannelboard. Use them while you tell the story.* *As you read, use hand gestures and theatrical voicing appropriate to the various parts of the story. Suggestions are included. Feel free to add your own ideas.*

Duck and Bear Go to the Movies

One day Duck and Bear were driving to town to see a movie.

(Place the car, duck and bear pieces on the flannelboard.)

Suddenly they heard a loud POP!

(Jump, as though startled.)

"Oh no," said Duck. "We have a flat tire. What should we do?"

(Use one voice for Duck's words and a different, deeper voice for Bear's words. Place the flat-tire piece on one wheel of the car.)

"Now we won't get to see the movie," sighed Bear.

"We can change the tire," suggested Duck. "Then we can still see the movie."

"We don't have a spare tire," complained Bear. "We won't get to see the movie."

"Isn't that our friend Chicken's house over there?" asked Duck. "We could go to Chicken's house and call Rabbit to fix the tire. We haven't seen Chicken in a long time. It will be fun to visit with her."

(Place the house piece on the flannelboard far from the car.)

"Chicken probably isn't home today," said Bear in a gloomy voice. "She probably went to town to see the movie." As Duck and Bear walked to Chicken's house, they heard birds singing and saw many beautiful flowers.

(Tilt your head as though listening to the birds. Sniff the beautiful flowers. Put birds and flowers on the flannelboard between the car and the house. Move duck and bear pieces near the flowers.)

"Listen to the birds singing. Look at the flowers, Bear," said Duck. "Aren't they beautiful? If we didn't have a flat tire, we wouldn't have noticed those flowers or heard the birds."

"Well, I guess they are pretty now," said Bear, "but soon the birds will fly south and the flowers will fade away."

"Look at those white, fluffy clouds. That one looks like a castle," said Duck as he pointed to the sky.

(Look up where the clouds would be. Point at the castle cloud. Put cloud patterns on the flannelboard.)

"If there are clouds, it will probably rain soon," said Bear.

When Duck and Bear arrived at Chicken's house, she was very happy to see them.

(Move duck and bear pieces to the house. Place the chicken pattern outside the house.)

"Hello, Bear. Hello, Duck. I'm really glad you came to visit. I'm making hickory-nut cookies, and I was hoping someone would stop by to share them with me."

"Oh, thank you, Chicken," said Duck. "I love fresh hickory-nut cookies. Do you like hickory-nuts cookies too, Bear?"

"No," said Bear. "I'd probably find a shell in my cookie."

(Make a face as though biting into a nutshell.)

Duck called Rabbit to come and fix the flat tire.

Duck had a great day. He didn't get to see the movie, but he had fun eating hickory-nut cookies and playing games with Chicken while they waited for Rabbit.

Bear sat under a tree all by himself. He didn't have any fun at all.

"Duck and Bear Go to the Movies" Flannelboard Patterns

duck

bear

flat tire

car

"Duck and Bear Go to the Movies" Flannelboard Patterns

cloud

house

birds

flowers

chicken

What Is an Optimist?

Time	Activity	Procedure
10 minutes	**Discussion/ Anchoring**	*Use the following questions for class discussion.*

1. Where were Duck and Bear going?

2. What happened on the way?

3. Who was the optimist, Duck or Bear?

4. Give examples from the story that show how Duck was an optimist.

5. Give examples from the story that show how Bear was not an optimist.

6. Who would you like more for a friend, Duck or Bear? Why?

7. Give an example of a time when you could be an optimist like Duck.

Extension Activities

Language Arts
- Ask children to draw pictures showing other adventures for Duck and Bear. Ask them to share their picture stories during circle time.
- Watch a Winnie-the-Pooh video that features Eeyore (*Winnie-the-Pooh and the Blustery Day* is one children particularly enjoy). At various parts, stop the video and ask, "Is Winnie-the-Pooh (or other appropriate character—Rabbit, Owl, Piglet, Eeyore, Tigger, Kanga, Roo, Christopher Robin) being optimistic?" Ask children to explain their answers.

Related Reading
Charlotte's Web by E. B. White (Harper, 1952).
Good Times on Grandfather Mountain by Jacqueline Briggs Martin (Orchard, 1997).
The Grouchy Ladybug by Eric Carle (Harper, 1977).

Winning Words: I Can

Materials

"Can You Do It?" song
(page 34)

art materials for
selected activities

Objectives: Children will explore the positive statement *I can.*
Children will gain self-confidence by realizing they can accomplish
almost anything with the right attitude.

Time: Approximately 15 minutes
*(Additional time may be needed depending on extension activities
selected.)*

Time	Activity	Procedure
2 minutes	Introduction	**Teacher:** "Words are important. Can you think of words that make you happy?" *Reward answers with positive responses, and write them on the board.* **Teacher:** "I have two very important words to share with you today. Let's read them together." *Write the words I CAN in large letters on the board. Read the words with children.*
3-5 minutes	Winning Words	**Teacher:** "I can! Those are good words. Those are words an optimist would say, aren't they? "There are many, many things you can do. Will you name some for me?" *List children's suggestions under the words I CAN. Encourage them to mention skills they have mastered, such as riding a bike, drawing, singing, skipping, and tying shoes.* *When you finish the list, reread each item, one at a time. Ask children to tell how they learned these skills.*

Winning Words: I Can

Time	Activity	Procedure
5 minutes	**Sing Together**	*Display a copy of the song "Can You Do It?" Sing the song to the tune of "Are You Sleeping?" Point to the words as you sing. Invite children to join you as you sing it together two more times.*
5 minutes	**Anchoring**	*Ask children to give examples of how a plan can help them accomplish things they wish to do.*

Extension Activities

Art
Give children drawing paper and crayons or markers. Ask them to draw pictures of themselves learning to do something new.

Social Studies
Encourage children to share their skills with partners, and teach one another. Cut out large stars from construction paper. When a child learns a new skill, present him or her with a personalized star to wear in class and take home. Write *(Child's name)* can *(skill)* on the star.

Tori can tie her shoes.

Related Reading
ABC I Like Me by Nancy Carlson (Viking, 1997).
A Duck So Small by Elizabeth Holstein (Little Tiger Press, 1998).
The Little Engine That Could by Watty Piper (Scholastic, 1973).
The Little Red Ant and the Great Big Crumb: A Mexican Fable by Shirley Climo (Clarion, 1995).

Can You Do It?

Sing to the tune of "Are You Sleeping?"

Can you do it?

Can you do it?

Yes, I can!

Yes, I can!

I can do it.

I can do it.

Here is my plan.

Here is my plan.

Winning Words: I'm Sorry

Materials

"I Am Sorry" song (page 37)

art materials for selected activities

Objectives: Children will explore the positive statement *I'm sorry.*
Children will talk about ways that working together can be a positive experience.

Time: Approximately 15 minutes
(Additional time may be needed depending on extension activities selected.)

Time	Activity	Procedure
2 minutes	**Introduction**	**Teacher:** "Today we will talk about other important words. Today's words are *I'm sorry.*" *Write I'M SORRY on the board.* **Teacher:** "Why do you think *I'm sorry* are important words?" *Wait for children's responses. Encourage them to give specific examples.*
7 minutes	**Sing Together**	*Display a copy of the song "I Am Sorry." Read the words with children. Sing the song to the tune of "Are You Sleeping?" pointing to the words as you sing. Invite children to join you as you sing it together.*
5–10 minutes	**Winning Words**	*Ask children to give examples of how saying "I'm sorry" can help people get along.* **Teacher:** "Should children be the only ones to say 'I'm sorry?' When might it be necessary for an adult to say 'I'm sorry' to a child? "Who can give me an example of how working together can make a group strong? Can you give me an example of how working together makes a job easier?

Winning Words: I'm Sorry

Time	Activity	Procedure
2 minutes	Anchoring	"Can you give me examples of how families work together? "Does working together have anything to do with sharing? Can you give me some examples?"

Extension Activities

Social Studies
- Elicit ideas for group projects that children can do in class, then assign small groups to each task. Emphasize that they are sharing the work.
- Remind children that it is important to be sincere and speak kind words. Have children work in pairs. The first child tells the other something good he or she knows about him or her. The second child thanks the first. Then children reverse roles. Model this activity first to make sure children understand.

Art
Give children drawing paper and crayons or markers. Ask them to draw pictures of themselves working together with friends or family members.

Related Reading
The Bundle of Sticks, a fable by Aesop found in many collections.

I Did, I'm Sorry by Carolyn Buehner (Dial, 1998).
It's Mine by Leo Lionni (Dragonfly, 1996).
Just Be Nice . . . and Say You're Sorry! by Catherine McCafferty (Golden, 1998).
Liking Myself by Pat Palmer (Impact, 1978).

I Am Sorry

Sing to the tune of "Are You Sleeping?"

I am sorry.

I am sorry.

I was wrong.

I was wrong.

Let's work together.

Let's work together.

Together we are strong.

Together we are strong.

Lesson 8

Winning Words: I Am Thankful

Materials

"I Am Thankful" song (page 40)

art materials for selected activities

Objectives: Children will explore the positive statement *I am thankful.*
Children will discuss reasons they have to be thankful.

Time: Approximately 15–20 minutes
(Additional time may be needed depending on extension activities selected.)

Time	Activity	Procedure
2 minutes	Introduction	**Teacher:** "We talked about the words *I can* and *I'm sorry* in our last two lessons. Today we have another phrase that is important. Today's words are *I am thankful.*" *Write* I AM THANKFUL *on the board.* **Teacher:** "Why do you think *I am thankful* are important words?" *Wait for children's responses. Encourage them to give specific examples.*
5 minutes	Sing Together	*Display a copy of the song "I Am Thankful." Read the words with students. Sing the song to the tune of "Twinkle, Twinkle, Little Star," pointing to the words as you sing. Invite children to join you as you sing it together two more times.*
5–10 minutes	Winning Words	**Teacher:** "According to the song, what should we be thankful for? "What else should we be thankful for?" *Children usually remember to be thankful for material things or physical attributes, but often forget about immaterial gifts, like the love of parents, friendship, and nature. As you talk about things to be thankful for, guide them to think of these ideas as well.*

Winning Words: I Am Thankful

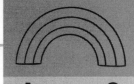

Time	Activity	Procedure
		Teacher: "Thanksgiving is a holiday when most people remember to be thankful. Is Thanksgiving the only day we should remember to be thankful?
2 minutes	Anchoring	"When is a good time to say the words *thank you?*"

Extension Activities

Art

• Give children drawing paper and crayons or markers. Ask them to draw pictures of themselves with things that they are thankful for.

• Invite children to cut pictures of things that they are thankful for from old magazines and catalogs. They can glue their pictures to construction paper. Use their artwork for a bulletin board display titled *We Are Thankful!*

Language Art

Ask each child to think of one thing for which he or she is thankful, but keep it a secret. Then have children take turns giving clues while the others try to guess. Model this activity first to make sure children understand.

Social Studies

Make badges for each child in the class from construction paper. Make the badge for each quality a different shape or color. Help children earn badges by announcing the quality at the beginning of the day. Write it on the board as a reminder. Concentrate on only one quality at a time. Give all children a chance to earn the badge for that quality before going on to the next one.

Possibilities for badges include:

_____ was friendly today.   _____ was helpful today.
_____ shared today.   _____ said kind words today.
_____ was thankful today.

Related Reading

I'm Thankful Each Day by P. K. Hallinan (Ideals, 1998).
The Mixed-Up Chameleon by Eric Carle (Harper, 1984).
Thank You, Pooh by Ronne Randall (Golden, 1996).

Lesson 8

I Am Thankful

Sing to the tune of "Twinkle, Twinkle, Little Star."

I am thankful for my life,

For the sun that shines so bright,

For the stars that twinkle at night,

For the trees, they're a beautiful sight.

Thank you, thank you for all I have.

I will remember when I'm happy or sad.

40

People Puzzles

Materials

Pictures 1, 2, 3, and 4
(pages 44–47)

art materials for
selected activities

Objectives: Children will examine facial features and note differences between happy expressions and grumpy expressions.
Children will learn that sharing is a positive experience.

Time: Approximately 20–25 minutes
(Additional time may be needed depending on extension activities selected.)

Time	Activity	Procedure
2 minutes	**Circle Time**	*Chant this poem of welcome while children gather for circle time.* **Teacher:** "Please come join the circle. Please come join the circle. Please come join the circle. You are important, every one."
5 minutes	**Introduction**	*Review the Magical Talking Stick Rules.* **Teacher:** "Faces can tell us a lot about what people are thinking. "Who remembers the word we learned for people who look for ways to be happy?" *Allow children to respond.* "Optimist! That's right. "Today we will look at some pictures and see who is being an optimist and who is not. Remember when we were Emotion Detectives? We will do that again today as we look closely at the faces of the children in the pictures."
10 minutes	**Discussion**	*Hold up the four pictures, one at a time. Use the discussion questions on page 42–43.*

People Puzzles

Display Picture 1 (page 44): Two girls are fighting over a toy.

1. What is happening in the picture?

2. Is there a problem?

3. What is the problem?

4. Do the girls look happy?

5. How can you tell from looking at their faces that they are not happy?
   (Encourage children to note facial features like raised eyebrows, eyes, wrinkled noses, down-turned lips, chins jutting forward, and hands clenched into fists.)

6. Are these girls being optimistic?

7. What do you think they could do to solve the problem?

8. How do you feel when you and a friend are able to solve a problem?

9. Would you like to be friends with the girls in this picture? Why or why not?

Display Picture 2 (page 45): Two girls are sharing a toy.

1. What is happening in the picture?

2. Is there a problem?

3. Do the girls look happy?

4. How can you tell from looking at their faces that they are happy?
   (Encourage children to notice the expression in the eyes, the up-turned lips, and the arms open to each other.)

5. Are these girls being optimistic?

6. Are they sharing? Is sharing something that happy people do?

7. Sharing isn't always easy. When could it be hard to share?

8. Would you like to be friends with the girls in this picture? Why or why not?

Display Picture 3 (page 46): One boy made a big mess. The other boy is angry and wants him to clean it up.

1. What is happening in the picture?

2. Is there a problem?

3. What is the problem?

4. Do the boys look happy?

5. How can you tell from looking at their faces that they are not happy?
   (Encourage children to notice facial features similar to those in Picture 1.)

6. Are these boys being optimistic?

People Puzzles

7. What do you think they could do to solve the problem?

8. How do you think they would feel if they solved the problem?

9. Would you like to be friends with the boys in this picture? Why or why not?

Display Picture 4 (page 47): Two boys are helping each other clean up a big mess.

1. What is happening in the picture?

2. Is there a problem?

3. Do the boys look happy?

4. How can you tell from looking at their faces that they are happy? *(Encourage children to notice facial features similar to those in Picture 2.)*

5. Are these boys being optimistic?

6. Are they sharing? If so, what are they sharing?

7. Would you like to be friends with the boys in this picture? Why or why not?

Time	Activity	Procedure
5 minutes	**Anchoring**	*Place all four pictures on display. Use the following questions to summarize the lesson.*

1. Which picture would you like to be in? Why?

2. Which picture would you *not* like to be in? Why?

3. *(Point to Pictures 1 and 3)* If you act like the children in these two pictures, how do you think other people will feel about being your friend?

4. Does your face tell other people when you are happy?

5. Does your face tell other people when you are optimistic?

Lesson 9

     reproducible

Lesson 9

reproducible

Extension Activities

Art

Write the following words on the chalkboard:

book	6 toys	apple	dog	3 cookies
movie	big mess	backseat	hug	swing

Read the words to children. Ask them to draw a picture showing how two people could share one of the items listed.

Language

• Have each child cut a picture of a person from an old magazine. (If you prefer, you may provide the pictures.) Ask children what they think the expressions on the people's faces tell about how they feel. Have children look for clues in the pictures to find out what may have prompted these particular emotions. At circle time, have children take turns telling stories about the people in their pictures.

• Use a picture of a person with very expressive facial features as a story starter. Have children sit in a circle. Start the story, then go around the circle asking each child to add one sentence to the story. Tape-record or write the story as it's told. Print the story on chart paper and read it to the children the next day.

Math

Sharing problems make perfect math story problems. Use those listed below as examples. Make up your own using the names of children in the class. Have children make up sharing story problems and work them out with partners. Encourage children to use manipulatives to work out the answers.

"Kristen has four cookies. If she and her brother share the cookies equally, how many cookies will each one get?"

"Dad gave Todd ten marbles to share with his sister. How many marbles will each one get if Todd shares evenly?"

"Jason's friend wants to play with some of Jason's toy cars. If Jason has eight cars, how many will each boy have if they share equally?"

"Maria has six friends over for her birthday party. There are 14 balloons. How many balloons will each child receive if they share equally?"

Related Reading

Let's Care About Sharing by P. K. Hallinan (Ideals, 1997).
Little Brown Bear Learns to Share by Claude Lehun and Danielle Bour (Children's Press, 1997).
Oh, Bother! Someone Won't Share! by Betty Birney and Nancy Stevenson (Golden, 1993).

Laugh a Lot

Objective: Children learn that laughter can help get rid of the "grumpies."

Time: Approximately 15 minutes
(Additional time may be needed depending on extension activities selected.)

Materials

"Magical Talking Stick Rules" (page 14)

"I Can Make Me Laugh" chant (page 51)

art materials for selected activities

Time	Activity	Procedure
1 minutes	**Review**	*Welcome children into a circle. When they are settled, review the Magical Talking Stick Rules.*
2 minutes	**Introduction**	*Draw two very large trees on the chalkboard, one with leaves, the other with leaves and apples.* **Teacher:** "Do you think trees are funny? Do they make us laugh?" *Allow children to respond.* **Teacher:** "You're right. Trees are not funny. They are beautiful. Some trees have leaves. Some have flowers. Some have fruit, like apples, pears, and plums. "What if we were in a grumpy mood and wanted to get rid of our grumpies? Maybe we could do it by thinking of something funny." *Point to the trees.* **Teacher:** "What about if we thought about trees in a different way? Could they be funny? Let's find out by playing a game called *I Can Make Me Laugh a Lot*."

Laugh a Lot

Time	Activity	Procedure
3 minutes	**Chant**	*Display a copy of the chant "I Can Make Me Laugh." Point to the words while you chant them once. Then have children join you to chant it several more times.*
5 minutes	**Share Ideas**	**Teacher:** "Let's play the game now. What could we pretend grows on trees that would be funny or unusual?" *As children respond, let them draw the items on one of the trees. Comment positively on their ideas:* "Wow! That would certainly be strange!" *or* "I never thought of that growing on a tree!" *or* "An umbrella tree! That's a funny idea." **Teacher:** "Some of your ideas are really funny. They make me laugh a lot. What do you feel when you laugh at something funny? "Do you laugh just with your face? "How does your whole body laugh?" *Encourage children to mention how their stomachs shake, their eyes widen, giggles explode from their mouths, and so on.*
3 minutes	**Anchoring**	**Teacher:** "Laughing makes you feel good all over doesn't it? "If you are having a grumpy day, do you think laughing could help? "Maybe that would be a good idea. When you're having a grumpy day, try thinking about something odd or funny that could grow on a tree. It might help turn your grumpy face into a smiley face."

Name _____

I Can Make Me Laugh

When I'm feeling sad

Or a little bit mad,

Good humor and jokes

Can help me feel glad!

   © Fearon Teacher Aids FE11026

Extension Activities

Art

Invite children to come up with funny ideas for what unusual or fantastic things could grow from trees. Have them draw pictures of their funny trees and then title them, such as *Shoe Tree, Doll Tree,* and *Hamburger Tree.* Display children's artwork on a bulletin board titled *A Funny Forest.*

Math

Encourage children to count the number of items on their trees and write the numbers on the back of their papers.

Language Arts

• Provide plenty of riddle and joke books for children to giggle through. Ask them to share their favorites with the class.

• Invite children to make up their own riddles and share them with the class.

• Ask children to brainstorm words similar to *laugh.* List these words on the chalkboard. Title it *Laughing Words.* Some words, like *giggle,* almost seem to be laughing when you say them. (Use these words to supplement the list if children haven't already mentioned them: *giggle, chortle, silly, chuckle, guffaw, cackle, funny, comical, joyful, happy, merrymaking, rejoicing, smile, grin, gladness.*)

Related Reading

ABC Animal Riddles by Susan Joyce (Peel Productions, 1999).
Beastly Riddles: Fishy, Flighty, and Buggy, Too by Joseph Low (Macmillan, 1983).
The Carsick Zebra and Other Animal Riddles by David Adler (Bantam, 1983).
Elephants Never Forget! A Book of Elephant Jokes by Diane Burns (Lerner, 1987).
The Upside-Down Riddle Book by Louis Phillips (Lothrop, 1982).

Dessert Duos

Objective: Children explore humor as they work with partners to create unusual, funny desserts.

Time: Approximately 30–35 minutes
(Additional time may be needed depending on extension activities selected.)

Materials

"I Can Make Me Laugh" chant (page 51)

art materials for selected activities

Time	Activity	Procedure
3 minutes	Chant	*Display a copy of the "I Can Make Me Laugh" chant. Begin chanting while children gather in a circle. Use your happy voice. Invite children to join with you to chant the words a few times.*
1 minutes	Introduction	**Teacher:** "In our last lesson, we played the game *I Can Make Me Laugh a Lot.* Did you like that game? How would you like to play it again today?
13 minutes	Dessert Duos	"What if desserts grew on trees? Wouldn't it be nice if you could pick a chocolate sundae from a tree and eat it right now? What kind of desserts would you pull down from a dessert tree?" *Allow several children to reply.* **Teacher:** "All your good ideas are making me hungry. Too bad it's not time for dessert right now. "Desserts growing on a tree would be fun. But what if the desserts were not the usual kind? What if the desserts were funny?

Dessert Duos

Time	Activity	Procedure
	Dessert Duos (continued)	"Think of foods that just do not go together, like sour pickles and chocolate syrup, or apples and ketchup, or frosting and mustard." *Wrinkle your nose or make a "yucky" face to show what you think of those food combinations.* *Give children a chance to respond with their own weird food combinations.* **Teacher:** "Your ideas are wonderfully weird and very funny. Let's all work with partners to make up very funny desserts."
5 minutes	**Think and Plan**	*Divide children into pairs.* **Teacher:** "Before we start, can you give me some ideas about how we can share when we work with partners?" *Encourage children to suggest sharing ideas, such as sharing the time so both children get to talk, and talking quietly so they don't disturb others.* **Teacher:** "Work with your partner to make up a dessert we could serve that would have the strangest combination of food you can think of. Remember, everything in the dessert needs to be edible except the plate. "Plan a delightful dessert you can draw and share with the class. You can mix together as many foods as you wish to make your surprise dessert." *Let partners talk together to come up with ideas for silly desserts.*
5–10 minutes	**Drawing**	*Hand out crayons, markers, and a sheet of paper to each pair.* *As partners draw their creative concoctions, go from group to group, laughing and commenting on the different food combinations.*

Dessert Duos

Time	Activity	Procedure
5 minutes	**Presentation**	**Teacher:** "Now we are going to share the desserts we created. I had fun looking at many of your drawings and listening to you sharing your ideas while you worked. "You and your partner can share your ideas with the rest of the class. Remember, both of you shared ideas to make up this dessert and you can both share the time to present it to the class." *Call on groups to show their pictures and tell what strange combinations of food they used to create their delightful desserts.*
2 minutes	**Anchoring**	**Teacher:** "What made us laugh about these desserts? "Even though we would not want to really eat any of these desserts, they were fun to create. We all had good laugh playing the *I Can Make Me Laugh a Lot* game today. "We can think of other funny things to cheer ourselves up besides strange things growing on trees and weird food combinations for desserts. How about funny ways to travel? Or funny ways to wear our clothes? There are lots of funny things we can imagine to make ourselves laugh a lot. "Let's finish today's lesson with our chant." *Repeat the chant with children.*

Extension Activities

Art

• Ask children to make up names for their creative desserts and write them on the papers along with their names. (They can add the words: *Created by chefs . . . and . . . .*)

Make copies of all the artwork so each child has a copy of every dessert. Children can staple the pages together with construction-paper covers to make their own cookbooks. Ask them to make up appropriate names for the class books and write them on the covers. They can decorate the covers and take their cookbooks home to share with their families.

• Have children work together in pairs in the same manner as they did to create their delightful desserts. This time they can create new animals by combining several features from different animals into new creatures. Encourage them to make up names for their new animals.

Science

Many real plants and animals look like they got mixed up a bit. A kangaroo seems to have a face like a sheep, a pocket like a jacket, oversized feet, and tiny hands. Provide nature books with pictures of other "strange" animals and plants, like the platypus, horseshoe crab, or venus flytrap. Tie in this lesson with a science nature unit.

Social Studies

• Have children draw pictures of their neighborhoods, but ask students to change several things so they aren't quite the way they should be. Have children work with partners to find how many things are wrong in the pictures.

• Another option is to have students draw hidden objects in their neighborhood pictures, and challenge partners to find the hidden objects.

Related Reading

Duck, Duck, Goose? by Katya Arnold (Holiday House, 1997).
I Want to Be Somebody New! by Robert Lapshire (Random, 1986).
The Mixed-Up Chameleon by Eric Carle (Harper, 1984).
Oscar's Spots by Janet Robertson (Bridgewater, 1993).
Very Mixed-Up Animals: Mix and Match More Than 1,000 Weird Animals by Ian Jackson (Millbrook, 1998).

Cheery Chums

Objectives: Children will compare attitudes of characters in a puppet show and determine which are optimists.

Time: Approximately 15–20 minutes
(Additional time may be needed depending on extension activities selected.)

(For this lesson, have three older students or volunteers present the puppet show. To get the right attitude and meaning across, they need to be expressive readers. They will need copies of the script in advance and time to rehearse.)

Materials

3 hand puppets—Cheery Chums Ben, Tina, and Hope. (These can be made from socks or paper bags.)

puppet stage (This could be a table covered with a white sheet.)

Copies of "Cheery Chums Script" (pages 59 and 60)

Winning Words songs:
"Can You Do It?" (page 34)
"I Am Sorry" (page 37)
"I Am Thankful" (page 40)

art materials for selected activities

Time	Activity	Procedure
2 minutes	Circle Time	*Chant the poem of welcome while children gather for circle time.* **Teacher:** "Please come join the circle. Please come join the circle. Please come join the circle. You are important, every one."
2 minutes	Introduction	**Teacher:** "Today we are going to watch a puppet show called *Cheery Chums.* Who knows what the word *chum* means?" *Allow children to respond.* **Teacher:** "That's right, *chum* is another word for *friend.*"
10 minutes	Puppet Show	*Have your volunteers present the puppet show.*
5 minutes	Anchoring	*Use the questions on page 58 for group discussion after the show.*

Discussion Questions

1. Was Ben an optimist at the beginning of the play?

2. Why was Ben upset?

3. Do you ever get upset?

4. Who helped Ben change and become an optimist?

5. Was Tina being optimistic at the beginning of the play?

6. Why was Tina upset?

7. Who helped Tina change and become more optimistic?

8. Was Hope an optimist at the beginning of the play?

9. Why is Hope a good name for that character?

10. What was Hope's plan?

11. What makes a Cheery Chum cheery and optimistic?

12. Who do you know that is a Cheery Chum?
    (Encourage children to give specific reasons for their answers.)

13. What can we do to become more optimistic in our lives?

14. How can we get started?

15. What's our plan?

Time	Activity	Procedure
1 minutes	Follow-up	**Teacher:** "Which of our Winning Words songs would you like to sing today to help you remember the puppet show? 'Can You Do It?,' 'I Am Sorry,' or 'I Am Thankful'?" *Display the words to the chosen song and sing it with children.*

Cheery Chums Script

Teacher: Welcome to our play. I would like to introduce you to my three Cheery Chums: Ben, Tina, and Hope.

(Point to each volunteer as you say his or her stage name. He or she can acknowledge the introduction by having the puppets take a bow.)

(The play begins with the Ben puppet alone on the stage.)

Ben: Hello. My name is Ben. I haven't been a Cheery Chum very long, but I am now. I didn't believe in being optimistic, in working hard, in making a plan, in saying "I'm sorry," or being thankful for all that I have. I always felt angry that other children had more toys and things than I did. It seemed so easy for them to be happy. It seemed that they had such a good life. I wanted what they had until I met Hope and Tina.

(Ben moves to the side of the stage. Tina and Hope appear on the stage.)

Ben: I was walking to school one morning, feeling very jealous of Darryl, a boy in my class who seems to have everything. The day before, he showed me his awesome new toys. I was feeling rotten because he got the toys I wanted. I looked up and saw two girls. They were walking ahead of me and talking.

(Tina and Hope move to the front of the stage to deliver their speeches.)

Tina: I am so mad at Mom and Dad for arguing, especially today when it's our first day at a new school. We need to stick together in this house. I want to stay in this school. I don't want to move anymore. We moved five times in the last year.

Hope: You know Mom and Dad really love each other. It's just really hard right now because Mom lost her job. I heard them talking it out after their fight. Dad said he could get an extra job working part-time at night. I know we can help out too. Maybe we could deliver newspapers or help more around the house.

Tina: You know, Hope, that makes me feel a lot better. I was feeling angry and hurt, but I really like your plan. It shows we can do something to help. I know we need to appreciate what we have. Mom and Dad may be arguing now, but they always talk it over, make a plan, and before you know it, they apologize. I keep forgetting we have a nice place to live and good food to eat. I also have you, Hope. We're lucky and I'm thankful.

(Tina and Hope move back. Ben moves forward.)

Ben: When I heard Tina and Hope, I knew I had better rethink my attitude. I was not being very optimistic. Tina and Hope were thinking of things they could do to help. They had a plan. They were happy with their lives even if things were a bit bumpy right now.

(Ben walks over to Tina and Hope.)

Cheery Chums Script

Ben: Can I walk with you to school?

Hope: Sure. We're new here. It would be great if somebody could show us around. My name is Hope. This is my sister, Tina. What's your name?

Ben: My name is Ben. I'd like to be your friend.

(Tina, Hope, and Ben walk off together. Ben comes back alone.)

Ben: After I met Tina and Hope, I felt good. I knew I had found two Cheery Chums. I decided I was wasting my time being angry when I could be cheery like them.

(Tina and Hope return to the stage.)

Tina, Hope, and Ben: And that's how we became the Cheery Chums. We want to thank you for being our Cheery Chums, too. You were really quiet and such good listeners.

(The Cheery Chums bow and leave the stage.)

(Lead everyone in applause. Introduce the three Cheery Chums by their real names and thank them for doing a great job.)

Extension Activities

Art
- Have children draw pictures showing what they think the Cheery Chums might do in another situation. Ask them to share their pictures and ideas during circle time.
- Children can use white paper plates to make Cheery Chum faces and decorate them with crayons, paint, and markers. Display the Cheery Chum faces as a border along a wall in your classroom.

Language Arts
- Ask children to work in groups of three using the Cheery Chums puppets to make up their own short puppet shows. Invite them to present their plays to the class.
- Ask children to name characters in books, movies, or stories they have read who would be good Cheery Chums. Have them give reasons why these characters would be good Cheery Chums. Write the characters' names on the board. Have the class vote for the character they think would be the best Cheery Chum.

Math
Have children count the number of votes in the above activity and determine which character received the most votes.

Music
Divide children into three groups. Assign one of the Winning Words songs to each group. After they practice the songs and learn the words, they can present the songs to another class.

Social Studies
- Ask children to name family members, friends outside of the classroom, or community workers who would make good Cheery Chums. Have them give specific examples of why these people would be good Cheery Chums.
- Ask children to make a plan to welcome a new student (or practice teacher, guest speaker, and so on) into the class. Talk about how it feels not to have any friends and how children can share themselves to help someone new feel welcome.

Related Reading
The Best Baby-Sitter Ever by Richard Scarry (Aladdin, 1995).
How Pizza Came to Queens by Dayal Kaur Khalsa (Crown, 1989).
Together by George E. Lyon (Orchard, 1989).

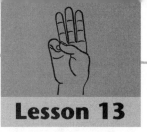

Lesson 13

Welcome to the Cheery Chums Optimist Club

Objective: Children will join the Cheery Chums Optimist Club and receive a certificate.

Time: Approximately 10–15 minutes

Materials

one copy of "Cheery Chums Optimist Club Pledge" (page 63) per child

one copy of "Cheery Chums Optimist Club Membership Certificate" (page 64) per child, filled out in advance

Winning Words songs:
  "Can You Do It?" (page 34)
  "I Am Sorry" (page 37)
  "I Am Thankful" (page 40)

Time	Activity	Procedure
2 minutes	Welcome	**Teacher:** "Today I want to invite you to become members of the Cheery Chums Optimist Club. This is a club for people who have learned to be optimists. "Would you like to join this club?
3 minutes	Introduction	"Members of the Cheery Chums Optimist Club make a pledge. A pledge is a promise." *Display the Cheery Chums Optimist Club Pledge. Point to each word as you read the pledge to children.* **Teacher:** "Do you think this is a good promise to make? Let's say the pledge together." *Read the pledge line by line. Pause after each line and ask the children to repeat it.*
7 minutes	Presentation	Invite children to accept their certificates, one at a time. Make the experience special by identifying one way each child has demonstrated an optimistic approach to life.
3 minutes	Conclusion	*Sing one or all of the Winning Words songs at the end of the presentation ceremony.*

Name _____

Cheery Chums
Optimist Club Pledge

I can work hard.

I can plan for good things to happen.

I can say I am sorry when I am wrong.

I can be thankful for what I have.

I know I can have a good life.

I can make my life better by being an optimist.

reproducible   © Fearon Teacher Aids FE11026   **63**

This is to certify that

_____

(child's name)

is a member of the

Cheery Chums Optimist Club

_____

(teacher's signature)

_____

(date)